THE ARTISTIC UNITY OF THE RUSSIAN ORTHODOX CHURCH

Religion, Liturgy, Icons & Architecture

THE ARTISTIC UNITY OF THE RUSSIAN ORTHODOX CHURCH

Religion, Liturgy, Icons & Architecture

Jane Merriam de Vyver

FIREBIRD PUBLISHERS
Belleville, Michigan

THANKS

Many thanks to Dr. Gloria House, Associate Professor of Humanties at Wayne State University, for providing the title and the opportunity to write and to present this study in her WSU Conferences on the "Sources of Artistic Inspiration."

Poems and photos
(except icons)
are by the author.

ISBN   1-881211-01-0

FIREBIRD PUBLISHERS
[a division of RUSSIAN TREASURES, INC.]
P.O. Box 303, Belleville, MI 48112

THE SOURCE OF BEAUTY

All beauty
Is a reflection
Of the divine Nature

All creation of beauty
Is an imitation
Of the divine Activity

All lovers of beauty
Are lovers of the Divine-
The source of all love and beauty

*1. **Cathedral of the Birthgiver of God**, Monastery of St. Tikhon, Zadonsk, Russia, 18th century; renovations, 1991.*

Typical of the thousands of the newly opened churches in the former Soviet Union is the partially renovated cathedral at St. Tikhon's Monastery in rural southwest Russia. Although the cathedral itself was returned to the Orthodox Church in 1990, a year later most of the small and modest monastery grounds were still being used as a factory. Located on the west bank of the Don River in the Voronezh Diocese, the once thriving monastery is home to a growing number of monks and novices. Monasticism has always played an extremely significiant role in the Russian Orthodox Church, and now many men and women of all ages are entering monastic life, an expression of the intense spiritual life of the Orthodox Church.

As is occurring everywhere in the former Soviet Union, the long, hard work of renovating the cathedral proceeds gradually. The former beauty slowly returns, as the exterior is restored and painted, and the barely discernible icons that had formerly covered the interior walls are painted anew.

CONTENTS

2. Holy Trinity-St. Sergius Lavra Monastery, Sergieev Posad (formerly, Zagorsk), Russia, 14th-20th centuries.

St. Sergius of Radonezh (ca.1314-1392) founded this monastery around 1334, deep in the forest about 45 miles northeast of Moscow. It has continued to be the most important monastery in Great Russia ever since. Not only has it been a spiritual, theological and artistic center, but its influence was felt politically through the spiritual guidance given by its abbots to the Grand Princes and Tsars of Moscow.

Located here today are an active monastery, and a major seminary and theological academy; until 1990, it was the residence of the Patriarch of Moscow, who now resides in Moscow. Every year thousands of pilgrims flock here for the feast days of the St. Sergius, whose tomb is in the Holy Trinity Church. It was for the tomb of his spiritual father that the great iconographer, St. Andrei Rublev, painted his famous icon of the Holy Trinity around 1411. The present stone church, constructed in 1422 to replace St Sergius' original wooden temple, is the oldest surviving building at the monastery.

1

THE ARTISTIC UNITY OF THE RUSSIAN ORTHODOX CHURCH

TRANSCENDENCE REVEALED

How dare we
Break into
Divine Silence
With our arrogant noise
When the beauty
Of a song, a dance
A flower, an icon -
Like the glee
Of a child at play -
Says more than
All the world's wise words
So solemnly pronounced

1

THE ARTISTIC UNITY
OF THE
RUSSIAN ORTHODOX CHURCH

The very prolific artistic production of the Russian Orthodox Church during the past 1,000 years reflects a unified spiritual and artistic vision. Russian religion, ritual, painting/writing of icons and architecture all spring from the same source, and all say the same thing. Even today, the newly revivified Russian Church continues to manifest the same artistic unity as it has for ten centuries. The source of the creative impulse for much of the abundant artistic production of Russia throughout the centuries is the spiritual vision of Russian Orthodox religion. All of the art forms participate in the celebration of joy and life and resurrection that forms the Russian Orthodox ritual - the Divine Service - which in turn is a visualization and embodiment of the religion.

Before trying to define Russian Orthodox religion, it is important to comment on the criteria used to define it. Although in times of theological controversy, Orthodox doctrines and dogmas have been of crucial importance (especially in the earlier centuries)

11

the Russian Orthodox Church generally prefers not to define itself solely by its dogmas. Instead, being more Eastern than Western in most ways, Russian Orthodox religion in practice has more to do with action than dogma. A believer is recognized more by living a Christ-conformed life, where Christ's moral precepts, particularly the corporal works of mercy, are taken very seriously, than by the cognitive content of the person's belief system. St. James' exhortation that faith without good works is dead and useless (James 2:14-26) has always been very alive for Russian Christianity. Is it accidental that the letter of St. James is the very first of the letters in the Russian New Testament, whereas it is one of the last letters in Western versions? For Russian Christianity, the faith that results in conforming to Christ is not focused on dogma, but on one's relationship with the Divine, including the divine within oneself, within others, and manifested throughout creation.

A corollary of the Russian Orthodox emphasis on faith as right relationship and right action rather than as dogma, is that instead of writing dogmatic theological treatises, the greatest genius of the Russian Church's theological expression is in the writing of theology with paint - icons - rather than with ink. It is significant that as soon as we begin to define Russian Orthodox religion, we immediately find ourselves talking about the arts, because the theology of beauty and the creation of beauty plays a crucial role in the Orthodox Church, and especially in the Russian Church. Orthodoxy without the arts would not exist. Without icons Orthodoxy would not exist.

The affirmation of the creation of beauty as an integral element of theology and sanctification is an expression of the Orthodox concept of the unity of life, and its rejection of excessive separation of life and humanness into intellect and emotion, mind and heart, mental and material, inner and outer being, spiritual and physical. To the Russian mind, a radical bifurcation of nature (such as tends to persist in the West) cuts us off from life: it results in the minimizing of the organic wholeness and unity of creation, of life and of the human person, that is so fundamental to the Russian Orthodox perspective. The physical and emotional realm is not to be deprecated as evil - as something from which to escape - but as that which is to become transfigured and spiritualized, as it participates in the process of sanctification. The popularity of the veneration of St. Seraphim of Sarov, whose body was transfigured as he participated in the *Uncreated Light of Mount Tabor*, is an example of this Russian Orthodox spiritual and theological precept.

Another preliminary consideration, before defining some principles of Russian Orthodox religion, is to mention the meaning of the word *Orthodox*. The Russian Orthodox Church is one of a number of nationally autonymous and autocephalous (self-governing) Eastern Orthodox Churches, that have their origin in the original Greek Orthodox Church. *Orthodox* means both *right worship/praise* and *right teaching*. Thus, the very name, *Orthodox*, speaks of the unity of teaching and action, faith and service, word and sacrament. While not being overly preoccupied with dogma, there is the lively recognition that our actions proceed from our beliefs. Thus, to act rightly, we must believe rightly. For Orthodox, right teaching is manifested and reflected in right living (conforming to the Image of Christ), and in right worship or ritual - the Divine Service - which utilizes all of the arts to perform its service, and is itself an art form.

**3. *Cathedral of the Savior, Savior-Andronikov Monastery,
Moscow, 1410-27(?), limestone.***

This church is one of the first stone buildings constructed in
northeast Russia after the Mongol Tartar invasion in 1238-40.
At the time the cathedral was built, the great iconographer, St.
Andrei Rublev, (d.1430) lived here. In recent decades the
Andrei Rublev Museum of Icons has been located at this fomer
monastery. In May 1991 the *Savior Cathedral* was returned to
the Church; the interior is totally bare, so it will take years to
fully restore.

Basic forms of traditional Russian Orthodox temple architecture are evident in this temple, especially the cross-in-
square cubical plan with triple apses, with a single central
dome. These forms are inherited from the pre-Invasion
Vladimir-Suzdal styles, along with other stylistic details.
Distinctive, however, are the lowered corners, the cascading
pointed (*ogee*) *kokoshniki* and *zakomara* roofs, which combine
to emphasize an upward central thrust.

The modest proportions and the simplicity and repetitve-
ness of the decoration reflect the 14th century's *hesychast* spirituality, which emphasized the ascent of the soul through inner
quieting, achieved by continuous 'prayer of the heart.'

2

PRINCIPLES OF
RUSSIAN
ORTHODOX CHRISTIANITY

DIVINE PARADOX

I. Truth revealed
    Truth reveiled
    Darkness illumined
    Light concealed
    Divine darkness
    Holy light

    Silence shouted
    Thunder whispered
    Transcendent appproached
    Uncontainable contained
    Divine paradox
    Holy wisdom

II. What is, is not
    What is not, is
    Dead are alive
    Living are dead
    Weak are strong
    Strong are weak
    Wise are fools
    Fools are wise

    More is less
    Less is more
    One is many
    Many are one
    Volumes say nothing
    Silence says all
    Divine paradox
    Holy wisdom

2

PRINCIPLES OF RUSSIAN ORTHODOX CHRISTIANITY

Of the major spiritual-theological-philosophical principles of Russian Christianity, we will identify thirteen, which are the artistic sources of Russian sacred arts. These principles are all interrelated, and essentially all proceed from the affirmation of God's creation of the world, and the Incarnation and Resurrection of Jesus the Christ; they are all firmly rooted in the Bible (such as Genesis 1-2 and Romans 8) and in the writings of the Church Fathers.

1. Sanctification of the material world

The material world, although fallen, is good, because God created it, and incarnated in it. Sanctified by creation and incarnation, the material world is called to participate in sanctification and be restored to its original beauty. This *high* conception of the physical world is an essential requirement for a theology of beauty and artistic creation. Whenever the physical realm is regarded as evil, base and corrupt, the arts diminish. For example, the sixteenth century Protestant reformer, John Calvin, rejected most arts, especially the visual, precisely because of his negative view of the body and all things physical.

17

This tradition continues to be strong in the United States.

2. We are icons of God

Humans are created in the Divine Image (*eikon* [icon] in Greek means *image*), and are called to restore the original beauty of that divine image and likeness, from which we have fallen away. This is an important biblical theme that recurs frequently. See, for example, 2 Corinthians 3:18, Romans 8:29, Galatians 4:19, and Ephesians 4:15.

3. Human nature is essentially beautiful, not corrupt

Unlike some western doctrines of the total depravity and debased character of human nature, Orthodox theology and spirituality regards human nature as beautiful, precisely because it is created by God in His own Image. Like a tarnished silver bowl, whose essential beauty can never be obliterated, but can be restored by polishing, so too our tarnished human nature can be, and is meant to be, polished and restored to its original beauty.

4. Participation of the cosmos in sanctification

When humans fell away from communion with God, the cosmos fell with them. Similarly, as the broken relationship between humans and the divine is restored, so too, the entire material realm is also restored. The whole creation groans in expectation of restoration (Romans 8:19-22). Humans, animals, nature and the whole of the cosmos are caught up in a process of conforming to the divine Image within us, which is a movement towards sanctification or deification (*theosis* in Greek), that is, becoming God or becoming like God.

5. Theology of Beauty

Eastern Orthodox Christianity is the only religion or Christian denomination that has a vigorous theology of beauty as a basic tenet. This proceeds from its *high* concept of the goodness and beauty of the material world and of human nature. There is the lively awareness that beauty imitates the divine nature; that to create beauty is to imitate the divine activity; and that to be a lover of beauty is to be a lover of God. The Resurrection or *Pascha* is called the "Pascha of Beauty" (*Paschal Verses*). At the end of the Divine Liturgy, there is a wonderful phrase in a prayer (*The Prayer before the Ambon*): "Sanctify those who love the beauty of Thy house." This reflects a distinctively Orthodox attitude towards the role of beauty in the spiritual life.

6. Humanity co-operates with God

Humans are called to work together with God in accomplishing the restoration of the cosmos to its original beauty. *Co-operate* comes from the Latin and *synergeia* is the Greek for *work together* - a central element of Orthodox and biblical spiritual theology. (See Romans 8:28.) Cooperating with God in the task of reconciliation of the world is part of what *divine service* is all about. It is precisely a result of the *high* concept of human nature as made in the divine Image, that humans are regarded as being capable of actually working together with God.

7. We stand in two worlds

The Kingdom of God is not just something that will appear at the end of time - it is already present and being manifested here and now. The icons, the church architecture and decoration, the liturgical music and the whole of Divine Service are a making present (re-presenting) of the divine realm - the ultimately Real world in whose midst we already stand. We stand in two worlds, with one foot in each - one foot in the Kingdom of God, and one foot in the temporal world that is in the process of being restored to the beauty of the divine Image.

8. Unity of life

While standing in two worlds, we experience the ultimate unity of opposites, unity of life, and unity of the cosmos; we experience the ultimate reality of the essential unity of the physical and the spiritual, the terrestrial and celestial, the human and divine. All of life is viewed as unified in its true essence. This concept of unity is related to reconciliation, so we speak of the reconciliation or unity of all seemingly opposed dimensions of life: unity of heaven and earth, visible and invisible, transcendent and immanent, spiritual and physical, Mind-Soul and body, the unity of God, and of humans with God, with nature, with the whole cosmos.

9. True life is tranfigured and resurrected

True life - real, rich life lived to the fullest - is a transfigured and resurrected life; it is life lived in the Divine Presence; it is life lived standing in two worlds. When they are being true to themselves, Russian

Orthodox arts and liturgy show forth that transfigured life and make present true reality as it is perceived with the inner eye - not with the outer eye.

10. Correspondence between earthly and heavenly realms

The concept of the unity of life spills over into two other areas: correspondence and paradox. Correspondence is very important in Russian Orthodox arts and ritual, where the physical and material liturgical acts and arts correspond to the spiritual and nonmaterial world. The earthly Divine Liturgy corresponds to its heavenly counterpart. The icon images of holy people and events correspond to the real person in the spiritual realm, and the cosmic-historic events that transcend time and history. The church building corresponds to the heavenly prototype, just as the Tabernacle of Moses, built according to its heavenly prototype, corresponded to it (Exodus 25:40). The concept of correspondence between the heavenly and earthly, and of following the heavenly patterns is a very strong motif in Hebrews, seen especially clearly, for example, in 8:5.

There is also much correspondence between the Hebrew and Greek (Old and New) Testaments. Virtually every act and concept of the Church and the New Testament has its Hebrew Bible (Old Testament) counterpart or prototype, to which it corresponds. The spiritual principle, "As above, so below," reflects this concept of correspondence, and is important in Orthodox church architecture, decoration and ritual. There is also usually the awareness that we are called to transcend and move beyond temporal manifestations, and ascend to the spiritual prototype - the ultimately Real world.

11. Paradoxical nature of Truth

The principle of the paradoxical nature of Truth is another fundamental element of the Orthodox ethos, although, as a cosmic truth, paradox is to be found in all great spiritual paths. The basic doctrines of Christianity are all paradoxical: God becomes man; a virgin gives birth; the immaterial becomes material; He who is beyond time and space and causality, comes into the realm of time and space and causality; more is less, and less is more; the dead are alive, the living are dead; standing in two worlds; unity of opposities - the list can go on and on. The very extensive *corpus* of Orthodox hymnography excels in the recitation of divine paradox.

12. Apophatic nature of Truth

Paradox is closely related to the apophatic nature of Truth. *Apophatic* means that the ultimate essence of the Divine and of divine Truth cannot be adequately apprehended by the human mind, nor adequately expressed in human words. Consequently, not dogmatic treatises, but a flower, paradox, silence, or an icon are regarded as being the most adequate ways of expressing the divine Essence. This Orthodox approach to Truth is in rather sharp contrast to the rationalistic tendency of Western thought, which tends to maintain that if something is true or real, then it can be apprehended by the mind, and explained through reason and logic.

13. Centrality of the joy of the Resurrection

The joy and glory of the Resurrection - the *Feast of Feasts* - is the single, pivotal, unifying experience of (Russian) Orthodox religion, and is reflected in all the art forms. Similarly, the divine and resurrected nature of Christ tends to be the Orthodox focal point, in contrast to the Western emphasis on Christ's Incarnation and Passion. In the Orthodox Church there are no *stations of the cross* to emphasize Christ's human nature and suffering. Instead, omnipresent icons proclaim the centrality of the resurrected, transfigured life of Christ, and life of the individual, the Church, and the cosmos conformed to Christ.

Liturgically, we see this Orthodox emphasis on Resurrection in many ways. For example, the most glorious of all the Gospel readings is the beginning of St. John's Gospel (the *Prologue,* John 1:1-17): "In the beginning was the Word, and the Word was with God, and the Word was God...." This is the Gospel reading for Pascha (Easter) for the Orthodox, whereas in the Western Church, it is the Gospel for Christmas Midnight Mass.

In the Orthodox Church, *the* midnight service - symbolically, the central liturgical enactment - celebrates the Resurrection of Christ; in the Western Church, *the* midnight service celebrates the Birth of Christ. In the Orthodox Church, even on the night of Holy and Great Friday (liturgically, Holy and Great Saturday), the awareness of the Resurrection is always present. After Christ's burial, in the Matins *wake* and in the Liturgy for Holy and Great Saturday, a wonderful hymn is sung, in which, speaking from the tomb, Christ says: "Do not lament for me, O Mother, seeing me in the tomb... For I shall arise and be glorified...." (Matins, *9th Ode*). Even the sadness of Great Lent and Holy Week is a *joyful sadness.*

This emphasis on resurrected glory, rather

than on human suffering, is never far from the Russian Orthodox consciousness. Perhaps it is precisely this vision of resurrected joy and beauty that has enabled the Russians to embrace suffering as part of the spiritual life - to endure so much suffering and still remain whole. Perhaps, too, it has helped to counterbalance the melancholy tendency of the Russian spirit.

The following story illustrates how fundamental to the Russian Orthodox way of life is the Resurrection - the glorious *Pascha of Beauty*. At a required meeting of all citizens in a Soviet village some decades ago, a state functionary delivered a several hour-speech on the 'glories' of atheism. Upon concluding, wanting to appear to be open, he offered the opportunity for anyone to refute what he had said. The quiet and reserved village priest stood up and declared in a strong voice: "Christ is Risen!" With one voice the entire village responded with a thunderous booming: "Truly He is Risen!" or "Indeed He is Risen!" (This is the dual exchange that is echoed repeatedly throughout the Pascha season.) In a single moment the hours of atheistic diatribes were invalidated. More was said in that single exchange than could have been said in hours of talking. Nothing more needed to be said.

We have seen how in even briefly defining the religion of the Russian Orthodox Church, we immediately had to speak of liturgy, beauty and the arts. What has been said above will now be expanded, with more explicit consideration of how Russian religion forms an artistic unity with its liturgy, icons and architecture, and how they embody these thirteen basic principles of Russian religion.

*4. Iconostasis, **Church of the Fathers of the Seven Ecumenical Councils**, St. Daniel's Monastery, Moscow; 1988 reconstruction, in the 15th century Moscow style.*

The iconostasis, a prominant characteristic of Orthodox churches, is a wall or screen of icons that separates the sanctuary from the nave. It is pierced by three doors: the double *Holy Doors* or *Royal Gates* in the center, behind which is the altar; and the Deacon's Doors to the sides.

Sanctuary screens were used in early Christian churches, but over the centuries the Slavic iconostasis grew higher and more elaborate, reaching five tiers in 15th century Russia. Later, it was ornately carved of wood and frequently gilded.

The meaning and function of the iconostasis includes: (1) salvation-history and the Kingdom of God, already manifested on earth in the Church and its liturgical life, are made visible and present realities; and (2) liturgical movement through the iconostasis and the opening/closing of the Holy Doors are important aspect of liturgical symbolism. When the clergy come through the Holy Doors to read the Gospel, preach the sermon, and bring Holy Communion to the people, it shows that God comes to us, penetrating the veil that separates heaven and earth.

5. *Reading the Gospel during Divine Liturgy, Theophany Pariarchal Cathedral, Moscow, 18th-19th centuries.*

The archdeacon (center) is about to read the Gospel. The subdeacons are carrying candles, symbolizing that Christ, whose message is proclaimed in the Gospels, is the Light of the World. The deacon in white holds the bishop's omphorion (stole), to signify that the deacon's authority to proclaim the Gospel is given to him by the bishop.

The Gospel is read in front of the iconostasis' open Royal Gates or Holy Doors, through which the altar is visible. The iconostasis is gilded carved wood. To the right of the Holy Doors is a large icon of Christ, and to the left is an icon of the Virgin Mary, usually called by the title, the "Birth-Giver of God." Notice the clergy's (gold) vestments, the beautiful rugs, candle-stands, brass railing, and lamps hanging in front of the icons. Visible in this photo is just a small portion of the very large iconostasis.

3

LITURGY

DIVINE LITURGY

Standing in two worlds at once -
The divine and the mortal -
We taste the incomprehensible
Sweetness and delight
Of offering divine service
Side by side with angels
Who serve invisibly with us
We taste Life
We embrace Life
We dance Life
Dancing in the Presence

3

LITURGY

Of central importance to the life of the Russian Orthodox Church is its worship, which is usually called *Divine Service*. So essential is it, that at times of persecution, the Church has survived as long as the Divine Service could be performed. Orthodox liturgical celebrations re-enact and make present the whole of salvation-history, inviting people's present participation in the past and future. Over and over the hymns for the feast days proclaim that *today* the events of salvation-history occur: *today* Christ is born; *today* is the beginning of salvation; *today* Christ is risen.

There is a great deal of ritual in Russian Orthodox life, at home and in the temple. The numerous ritual practices involve the offering of most every element and action of life to be blessed and sanctified. The major Divine Service is called the *Divine Liturgy* - which is the Orthodox counterpart to what other denominations call the Mass, Eucharist, Holy Communion, or Lord's Supper - within which the Mystery (Sacrament) of Holy Communion is received by the faithful. Since the times of the Apostles, the Church has been aware that it is being itself most when performing the Divine Service. The work of the Christian people is to offer divine service. The double meaning of the word *service* to refer to *serving* the needs of people, and *serving* the Divine Liturgy is significant: in serving God's creation, one offers worship; to offer worship to to serve and heal the broken world, the broken spirit. This is precisely what it is to participate in the joy and beauty of the resurrected life. This is Liturgy - this is the *work of the people* - (which in Greek, is precisely what the word *leiturgeia* [liturgy] means).

Orthodox liturgy is inconceivable without the arts in which it participates and through which it expresses itself: Liturgy itself is an art form. The ritual enactment of salvation-history that constitutes Orthodox Divine Service embodies all the arts: music, poetry, choreographed movement (dance), architecture, omnipresent icons, 'Persian' style rugs, the clergy's richly embroidered and decorated vestments made of exquisite fabrics, many sacred objects crafted from precious metals and stones (especially the Gospels-Book cover and Communion vessels), cut-glass chandeliers, the carved wood icon-screen (iconostasis) across the front of the church, plus folk arts, such as embroidered cloths around the icons and carved icon frames.

Surrounded by the beauty of all these art forms, the many candles' flickering flames and the hazy aroma of incense contribute to the spiritual, emotional, mental and physical experience of the beauty of the Divine Presence. When caught up in this experience, one joins with the Psalmist in singing, "Let my prayer arise in Thy sight as incense," (Psalm 143) as one's total being arises with one's prayer and is immersed in the Divine Beauty.

Is it any wonder that Prince St. Vladimir's emmissaries felt as though they did not know whether they were in heaven or on earth when they experienced the magnificent beauty of the Divine Services at the *Cathedral of the Holy Wisdom* (*Hagia Sophia*) in Constantinople? The Slavic love of divine beauty is reflected in this very story that Prince St. Vladimir chose Orthodox Christianity for his people one thousand years ago because of the awesome beauty. If there is something beautiful that can be crafted in words, music or materials, then it will be used in Orthodox Divine Service and to adorn the divine temple.

The reason for all these sumptuous art forms is most significant: Orthodoxy has a very rich awareness of the role and effect that beauty plays in human life. To be in the Divine Presence is to behold Beauty Itself - the source of all beauty. Beauty affirms the divinity of life and the potential that the human person can be restored to the divine Image. Life without beauty would be impossible. In the West we usually are so absorbed with what we call *practical,* that some people think that beauty is superfluous, unnecessary, impractical: money should be spent to feed people, not adorn churches. Orthodox Christianity in general, and the Russian Church in particular, lives the affirmation that beauty is indispensible and supremely practical: it provides a different kind of food, for in the midst of savage brutality, the beauty of a flower or icon can very literally save the soul. Dostoievsky reflects this Russian Orthodox spiritual perspective when he says in *The Idiot*: "Beauty will save the world." Furthermore, since the Christian temple or church building corresponds to the heavenly prototype, the dwelling-place of the Divine, it must be as beautiful as possible, to correspond to the Divine Beauty.

All Russian Orthodox liturgy is permeated by the experience of the correspondence between the liturgical acts enacted on earth and their heavenly prototypes. Not only do the deacons who serve at the earthly altar correspond to the angels who serve at the heavenly altar (frequently depicted in icons), but all the faithful who are praising God with hymns are viewed as representing the Cherubim who surround the throne of God, ever-singing, "Holy, Holy, Holy." This pivotal concept of correspondence is well expressed in one of the major hymns in the Liturgy, the *Cherubic Hymn*: "Let us who mystically represent the Cherubim, and who sing the thrice-holy hymn to the life-creating Trinity, now lay aside all earthly cares." After the Great Entrance, the hymn concludes: "That we may receive the King of All, who comes invisibly upborne by the angelic hosts." The reality of this invisible world inhabited by angels and saints and the "memory eternal" of the departed is of fundamental importance to Russian Orthodox religion, and its living experience that the whole cosmos - visible and invisible - participates in deification.

The Church's artistic creation of 2,000 years unites all those who have participated in the Church's liturgical life during those 2,000 years, as it unites the visible and invisible worlds, the temporal and eternal, the human and divine. One of the ways in which this paradoxical standing in two worlds is experienced liturgically is the overlapping of chanting and singing. For example, before the deacon or priest stops chanting, the choir is already singing its part in the great drama. This stereophonic overlapping also declares that time is transcended in the Kingdom of God.

*6. Altar, **Cathedral** of the **Protection** of the **Mother** of **God** (Pokrov), Voronezh, Russia.*

The altar is the most sacred place in an Orthodox temple. The square, free-standing altar is located in the center of the area behind the iconostasis, visible through the open Holy/ Royal Doors. Sometimes an icon of the Last Supper is on the front of the altar.

The altar is the throne of God and the tomb of Christ. Each time the Divine Liturgy is served on the altar, the birth, life, death and resurrection of Christ are made present realities. The altar is where God's Presence is manifested, and from which the Holy Light and Life-Creating Mysteries come forth - in the reading of the Gospel and in Holy Communion.

Among the few objects placed on the altar, the most important are the enthroned Gospels book and the Tabernacle, which contains the reserved consecrated Body and Blood of Christ. Under the Gospels is kept the *antimins.* This special cloth, upon which the Divine Liturgy must be served, is signed and given by the Patriarch or bishop who is responsible for the temple, and by whose authority the sacraments (Mysteries) are served.

7. A Child Receiving Holy Communion, Pokrov Cathedral, Voronezh.

In the Orthodox Church, infants receive Holy Communion immediately after being Baptized and Chrismated. It is the responsibility of the family and sponsors to bring children to Communion every week. Christ invites **all** to feast sumptuously at His banquet table, and He does not exclude children.

Both children and adults need spiritual food. The Orthodox Church maintains that it is not necessary to intellectually comprehend the Holy Mysteries (Sacraments) for them to be effective, any more than it is necessary to understand how physical food is digested in order to receive nourishment from it.

Before the people's Communion, part of the consecrated Body of Christ (leavened bread) is put into the chalice containing the consecrated wine - the Blood of Christ. The priest uses a small spoon to place both elements together into the mouth of each communicant. Assistants hold a red cloth under the chin to catch any spills.

In the Divine Service the abundant use of the material realm's most sumptuous and awesome creations is intended to overwhelm, for the beauty of God is overwhelming and awesome. This liturgical use of the material realm affirms its inherent goodness, and its participation in the sanctification and transfiguration of the cosmos. All the human senses are involved too, thereby, sanctifying them: incense - smell; receiving Holy Communion - taste; kissing icons, lighting candles, crossing oneself - touch; and the absolute banquet feast of sight and sound - the continuous *a cappella* singing and chanting, and all the abundance of the visual arts and action, amidst the flickering of candles and smoke of incense.

The many courses of banquet feasts are very long, and so are Orthodox Divine Services. The non-stop singing, the prolific poetry of the hymns, the plentiful liturgical action, all provide a wealth of food for the feast. This is true whether in a tiny parish in Siberia, Alaska or Michigan with a choir of two or three, or in a enormous parish in Moscow, Paris or New Jersy with a choir of thirty or forty, the banquet feast is still served. The banquet table is full-laden, and all are invited to feast sumptuously (*The Sermon of St. John Chrysostom*, Paschal Matins).

One might think that the length of Orthodox services precludes the very concept of the apophatic nature of Truth, of which we spoke above, where "less is more." However, the every extensive liturgical services instead speak of something else. They speak of the eternal and never-ending Divine Service - of being constantly in the presence of God, singing the continual divine praise. "Lord have mercy" is sung and chanted so often, it seems repetitious to some. But rather than the negative connotation of "repetitous," divine service is supposed to be "continuous."

8. Priest's vestments, embroidered by Mother Angelina, Yelets, Russia

These are beautiful examples of contemporary Russian vestments. Most vestments are made by nuns, and are genuine art treasures. Usually veiled in anonymity, the nuns are highly skilled artists, and their work is a real labor of love.

Shown here are details of the beaded embroidery on the upper back of a priest's *phelonion* - the long outer garment - (right), and an *epitrakhelion* - priest's stole - (left). Red glass beads form the center of each of the crosses on the *epitrachelion* and the horizontal band of crosses on the *phelonion*. The unusual large design of cross and flowers are formed by a mosaic of tiny colored beads: gold cross, red and pink roses, green leaves, and a blue anchor. The design symbolizes faith (the cross), hope (the anchor), and love (the red roses).

The Russian-style crown at the top is a *mitre,* which is worn by bishops, archimandrites and mitred archpriests. It has four small painted icons, one on each side, surrounded by gold embroidered leaves, against a blue velvet background. Shaped like the tsars' crowns, mitres represent the authority of those whose wear them - that they are rulers of the Church, as the tsars were rulers of the temporal realm.

The Orthodox take very seriously St. Paul's injunction to pray constantly (1 Thessalonians 5:17 and Ephesians 6:18); thus, the individual and the community all continually sing, chant or say "Lord have mercy," or the fuller version, known as the *Jesus Prayer*, "Lord Jesus Christ, Son of God, have mercy on me, a sinner." To have this prayer as one's constant companion, as faithful and continuous as one's heartbeat, is to live the *prayer of the heart*. When so lived, one approaches the ideal state of being, where there is no real line of demarcation between private and public, individual and corporate prayer - or between the eternal and temporal, immaterial and material, invisible and visible. Whenever anyone stands in the presence of God singing divine praises, he or she is surrounded by the whole host of angels and saints and spiritual beings who likewise are singing Divine Service and living a life of divine service.

9. *Yaroslavl Mother of God, Russian icon, 2nd half of the 15th century; in the Tretyakov Gallery, Moscow.*

The Orthodox Church offers special veneration to the Virgin Mary in role as the "Birth-Giver of God." She is a model of the Christian spiritual life and image of the Church, because, by her obedience to and cooperation with the divine will, the God-Man, Jesus, was incarnated. To affirm her role as the Mother of God, most icons of the Virgin portray her holding Jesus as the young Christ Emmanuel. She is usually dressed in a simple and modest maphorion. Christ is never portrayed as a helpless, naked baby, as He is in non-Orthodox religious painting, but as the fully-clothed Eternal Word and Wisdom of God Incarnate.

In this very popular "loving-kindness" (*eleousa* in Greek; *umileniye* in Russian) icon type, there is a profound human tenderness between Mother and Child, without becoming sentimental. The Birth-Giver of God looks over the head of Christ with a meditative expression, full of compassion for the world's suffering. She foresees her divine Child's mission, and that her heart will be pierced also. Mere human sentiment is transcended, and her love, compassion and meditation assume a cosmic dimension.

4

ICONS

HOLY ICON, SACRED IMAGE

Holy icon, sacred image
Vision of beauty divine
In whose image we were formed
Vision of human nature
Restored to its original beauty

Holy icon, sacred image
Vision of reality true
Wherein we perceive our true selves
Vision of our inner being
Restored to its primal purity

Holy icon, sacred image
Vision of life transfigured
Where love overpowers darkness
Vision of the light of life
Filling all creation with joy

4

ICONS

Icons are the sacred images of the Orthodox Church (used also by Byzantine Catholics). Icons can be of any size, and made of almost any material. Icons are absolutely esssential to Orthodoxy, as an affirmation of the Incarnation of Christ, of the goodness of the material world that God created, and of its potential for being transfigured as it participates in the restoration of humanity to the beauty of the divine Image and Likeness.

We mentioned at the beginning of this study that the greatest genius of the Russian Church's theological expression is in the writing of theology with paint rather than with ink. It is important to understand that the writing of words and the writing of images are seen by Orthodoxy as one and the same activity: *icons are silent sermons uttered in color.* The spirit of this awareness is akin to the story of the Buddha being asked to preach to his followers - and he silently held up a flower. He thereby said more than volumes of words could have said; by saying nothing, he said everything. Icons are like the Buddha's flower.

Recognizing Orthodoxy's belief in the paradoxical and apophatic nature of Truth leads us to realize that icons, like the Divine Liturgy, do what theological treatises cannot do. They put us into the Divine Presence and put the Divine Presence into us, and they proclaim the Divine Reality in "words and images" (*Kontakion* for Orthodoxy Sunday).

Both Greek and Russian word-use reveal the awareness of the similarity between the creation of words and images: the same word (*pisat* in Russian, and *grapho* in Greek) means both *to write* and *to paint*. Iconography (*ikonographia*) means both to *write* and to *paint* images or icons. This is why Orthodox will frequently say in English that icons are *written*. However, words and images are both painted and written: we *paint* images with words, and we *write* images with colors. Poets excel in painting images with words, but those who write images with colors are also poets. The Greek word, *poiesis,* from which our words *poet* and *poetry* are derived, refers to the creative activity. In the Greek translation of the Hebrew Bible (the *Septuagint*), it is this very word, *poetry*, that is used to describe God's act of creation (in Genesis 1 and 2, especially 1:1, 26, 27, 31). Again, this is the word used in the Letter to the Ephesians (2:10), which the *Jerusalem Bible* aptly translates into English: "We are God's work of art."

Thus God is recognized as the prototype of all poetry, of all artistic creation. He is the great Player; His activity is the great *Dance of Creation.* This is all part of the Orthodox Church's rich theology of beauty and theology of icons. Icons are the Orthodox Church's poetry written with paints, which are a result of the cooperation (by means of artistic and spiritual inspiration) between the iconographer and the sacred subjects depicted in the icons.

10. The Ascension of Christ, Russian icon, late 15th century.

Represented in this icon-poem written with colors and images are the Apostles, somewhat disarrayed, standing on the Mount of Olives, watching Christ ascend into the heavens, encircled in a cloud of glory, escorted by two angels. Two other angels are speaking to the Apostles. Unlike most icons, the Apostles are purposely shown disarrayed and confused, without halos, in profile and with their hands upstretched. This is to indicate that the Holy Spirit had not yet descended to enlighten them and empower them with peace, unity and wisdom. In contrast to the Apostles, however, the Mother of God (with a halo) stands in the center, directly under Christ, joining heaven and earth; as the image of the Church, she is perfectly serene and calm, with her hands raised in prayer.

The spiritual meaning of the Ascension and its icon is that we are to ascend with Christ and be united with the Father, and be constantly in the state of expectation of being filled with the Holy Spirit; it means that we are to join with the Apostles who, filled with joy, were continually praising God, united in prayer with the Mother of God and the other saints. (See Acts 1:6-14 and Luke 24:44-53.)

11. *Resurrection Christ, Russian icon, 15th century.*

The icon of the Resurrection does not depict what may have been observed with the physical eyes, but corresponds to the theological and spiritual meaning of the *Feast of Feasts*. Thus, the icon does what the Feast itself does: it transcends time and space, and reveals the cosmic meaning of salvation-history. The icon is a visual poem of the Paschal *troparion* hymn: "Christ is risen from the dead, trampling down death by death, and upon those in the tombs bestowing life."

Christ is portrayed in hell, surrounded by a triple-ringed glory, trampling down the gates of hell, and raising up Adam and Eve (representing all men and women), into the new, resurrected and transfigured life. Christ grabs Adam (and Eve, in some icons) by their wrists, rather than by their hands, to indicate that people resist being born again, and are resurrected by the power of Christ, not by human strength.

Flanking Christ are Old Testament saints and prophets who had announced the coming of the promised Messiah. Christ's garments flutter out as though in the wind, to symbolize that He is filled with the Holy Spirit. Beneath Christ, in the black hole of hell, is the Devil, who has been captured and rendered powerless - death trampled down by Christ's death. The divided mountains that touch the heavens, with Christ in between, symbolize the reconciliation of the cosmos to God.

It is important to recognize that icons cannot adequately be studied simply as 'art historical' objects. Ubiquitous icons are central to the life of Russian Orthodox people. They are found in every room of the home (a small temple itself), and everywhere in the temple. There is no such thing as having too many icons: too many icons would be like having too much life or joy or peace or love.

The study of icons cannot be separated from the liturgical, devotional and theological functions of icons. As explained by St. John of Damascus and St. Theodore the Studite during the Iconoclastic Controversy of the eighth and ninth centuries, icons proclaim and affirm the same Beauty and Truth as are found in the Gospels and the Cross.

Icons may be defined as glimpses of what is ultimately meaningful in life, and are mirrors of our true nature, our true selves. They are two-way windows into Ultimate Reality. They make present the Divine Kingdom, already made manifest here and now. They make visible the invisible, and are vehicles of the divine self-manifestation. They are instruments of grace, whereby persons can encounter God, Christ, the Saints, and enter into the present reality of sacred history as cosmic events that transcend time and space. They enable us to stand in two worlds, as they make present historic persons and events, but in a manner whereby they transcend history and reveal the cosmic significance of salvation-history. In icons, as in the Divine Services, we are not spectators, but participants in the vision of the reconciliation of the cosmos to God, and of the vision of who and what we are, why we are here on earth, and how we are to live our lives. Icons answer all our basic human questions: they reveal to us the face of humanity, the true visage of being human. Icons do all the same things as the Divine Liturgy does.

Of the many elements of the very complex language of iconography, we will examine six, to see the means by which the distinctive vision of icons is proclaimed.

1. Style

In order to manifest the nature of the transfigured life - life lived continually in the Divine Presence - the painterly style of icons must be transfigured. This is why authentic icons *look funny*. Some people say that the style of icons is not *realistic*, meaning thereby - "not duplicating the way in which we perceive the physical world." Orthodox theology, however, maintains that icons, like Liturgy, *do* depict the Real world - the divine Reality. Icons portray not what we see with our outer eyes, but with our inner eye, our *third* eye. Therefore, authentic iconographic style should not seek to imitate the way we see with our outer eyes, because then the theological and spiritual message is clouded. Humans, animals, architecture, rocks, mountains and trees - all are to be portrayed in a transfigured, non-illusionistic style, because all the cosmos participates in the restoration, just as all suffered the result of humanity's falling away from the divine Image and Likeness.

2. Light

The source of light in icons should not be an external source, which casts shadows; rather, light should bathe the entire surface evenly. Darkness, shadow and black are symbols of life lived without God; in the Divine Presence there can be no darkness (Rev. 21:23, 25; 22:5). Thus black is used in icons

12. Transfiguration of Christ, icon by Theophanes the Greek, ca. 1403, at the Tretyakov Gallery, Moscow.

The Transfiguration of Christ on Mount Tabor occupies a prominant and essential place in Orthodox theology and spirituality, and in the theology of the icon.

This biblical event affirms: (1) that God incarnated in Jesus the Christ; (2) that the divine Glory was visibly manifested in Christ; and (3) that the material world participates in sanctification.

Around Christ is a brilliant six-pointed "Glory," and a three-part circle, which represents the cloud of the Presence of God. Both are filled with gold rays, emanating from Christ, like the rays of the sun. The bluish-white light of the "Uncreated Light of Mt. Tabor" reaches out and touches the three apostles (James, John and Peter), who are knocked to the ground by the overwhelming experience of seeing a manifestation of the Glory of God.

13. Crucifixion, Russian icon, late 14th century; in the Andrei Rublev Museum of Icons, Moscow.

Peace, harmony and tranquillity characterize the icon of Christ's Crucifixion, revealing His death as a victory, not a defeat. The symmetrical and simple composition, where everything extraneous is omitted; the soft earth-tone colors; the graceful curves of the bodies of Christ, the Virgin and St. John the Theologian; and the transfigured style are some of the techniques used to create the serene, quiet mood.

Although almost naked, Christ has a spiritual body. The black cave/grave, containing the skull of Adam, symbolizes that Christ - the new Adam - vanquishes the power of darkness (death and sin) that had held humans captive as a result of Adam (generic "man") disobeying Divine Law.

Corresponding to historical fact, the walls of Jerusalem are faintly perceptible behind the figures. However, because the event occurs *outside* the walls, it is revealed as a cosmic event that thus cannot be contained within any limiting boundaries. The walls further indicate that when we participate in the death (and Resurrection) of Christ, we are given the freedom and power to stand outside the limiting walls of the "world's" perspectives about Life and Reality.

only to represent the world separated from God. The greatest source of light is the golden sun. Therefore, Byzantine icons traditionally have gold backgrounds; Russian icons are more likely to have backgrounds of painted color that simulates gold, or sometimes a red background that simulates the intensity of the light and heat of the fire of the Divine Presence.

3. Composition, Colors, Mood

The composition and colors of icons should evoke a mood of peace, harmony, simplicity and tranquillity, because that is the nature of living the centered spiritual life; such are the characteristics of life restored to comm-union, at-one-ment with the Divine. Thus, *busy* compositions and colors are to be avoided, and relatively simple compositions, frequently symmetrical, are the norm. Compositition can communicate countless different things. For example, in most icons of events of Christ's life (the Nativity, Theophany, Transfiguration, Crucifixion, Resurrection, Ascension), the composition is divided in half, with Christ in the center. This makes the statement: Christ reconciles the divided world to Himself - to the Divine Image of which He is a manifestation. Concerning colors - a fairly limited palette is customary: red, green, yellow, ochre and brown are dominant.

4. Reversed Perspective

The use of what is called *reversed perspective* is characteristic of the language of iconography. It is the opposite, or reverse of *Renaissance perspective*. The latter seeks to create the illusion of three-dimensional space on a two-dimensional surface, as perceived through human eyes looking out. Thus, objects further away from the viewer are drawn smaller than objects in the foreground. This perspective reflects a view of reality that says the *observer* is the source of reality, because what is portrayed is from the observer's point of view. On the other hand, the 'reversed perspective' of authentic icons makes the statement that the viewer is the one being looked at - by those dwelling in the Real world of the divine realm - a world perceived by looking within, not without. Thus, it is objects in the foreground of icons that customarily are smaller than objects in the distance. Many times the whole issue of perspective - and time and space - is made mute by depicting figures standing against a solid background, as though they were suspended in time and space, which is precisely what they are.

5. Time and Space

Just as the limits of time and space are transcended in the divine realm and in the Divine Liturgy, so too are they transcended in icons. Sacred events or persons are not confined and limited to a single historic moment - they are cosmic. One way in which this is demonstrated is when more than one event is depicted as happening at the same time. This is seen in icons of the *Communion of the Apostles*, where Christ is giving the consecrated bread to six apostles on the left, while at the same time, He is giving the

14. Annunciation, Russian icon, 15th century; from the Intercession (Pokrov) Monastery, Suzdal.

"Rejoice, O Full of Grace, the Lord is with you," proclaims the Archangel Gabriel, as he greets the Virgin, and announces that the Son of God is to become her son. The Virgin's head is inclined and her hand raised, signifying her modesty and acceptance of the Divine Will. The dove represents the Holy Spirit descending upon her, while the cloud at the top signifies "the power of the Most High" covering her with its shadow. The cloth across the top indicates that historically, the event occurred indoors, since icons depict cosmic events as occurring in front of, not inside, structures. Barely perceptible in her hands is the true purple thread that the Virgin was spinning for the new temple veil.

Not only does the "reversed perspective" of the architecture declare that the Wisdom of God reverses human perspectives, but the architecture here is totally illogical: the proportions of the windows and doors render them totally unusable, and the canopy and its support could not possibly stand up. This illogic expresses Divine Paradox: a Virgin gives birth; God becomes man; the Eternal Creator is born in time as a creature; the Virgin becomes a living Temple of God.

15. *Nativity of Christ, Russian icon, 16th century, from the Nativity Cathedral, Suzdal.*

The icon of the Nativity makes visible the incomprehensible mystery and divine paradox of the Incarnation of God. The mountains touch the heavens, showing that heaven and earth are united. The Divine Light comes from the cloud of the Divine Presence and penetrates into the darkness of the cave, at whose mouth Christ lies, affirming that Christ is the Light that shines in the darkness of the world. The "dumb" ox and ass are at Christ's side, for they recognize their Master (see Isaiah 1:3). The Lord's "manger" is a sarcophagus (coffin), and He is lying in it as though in His tomb, declaring that the purpose of Christ's Incarnation was to overcome death by His death.

In the center lies the Virgin - the Cherubic throne - who gave birth to the Transcendent One. In the upper left, angels offer praise; below them, the three magi follow the star. In the upper right, an angel announces the glad tidings to the shepherds, who are below. Across the bottom, two scenes affirm Christ's dual Nature as the God-Man: on the left, the devil (disguised as a shepherd) is tempting St. Joseph to think that Christ is only human, and not divine; and on the right, the mid-wives are giving Christ His first bath, signifying that Christ is not only divine, but also human.

consecrated wine to six apostles on the right. Similarly, in some *Nativity* icons, Christ is depicted in the center lying in the manger- sarcophagus, wrapped in swaddling clothes, while at the same time, in the lower corner, He is shown being given his first bath by the mid-wives.

Just as time is transcended in icons, so is space. People who do not understand icons, sometimes say that they are flat, because they do not have the illusion of three-dimensionality. On the contrary, the three-dimensional space *is* there, but it is the opposite of how we perceive space in the physical world. The space in icons is between the viewer and the background, especially when reversed perspective is emphasized. In Byzantine churches the architectural space is frequently incorporated as a part of the iconographic space in front of the surface of the icons.

6. Correspondence

Icons *correspond* to the historical person or event portrayed - they are not painted from the imagination. Thus, the persons and events are always identified by name (although sometimes in old icons the names are worn off). Yet, they also correspond to the cosmic reality of the Kingdom of God, and thus, they transcend history: a cosmic event cannot be confined or limited to a single historical moment. This theological perspective is reflected in icons by placing a cosmic event *outside*, not *inside* a structure. In icons of Christ's Nativity, Christ lies not *in* a cave, but at its mouth - illuminating the darkness, but not being confined by it. Events that occurred indoors historically, such as the Annunciation, Last Supper or Presentation of Christ in the Temple, are depicted in *front* of, not *inside* an architectural background; a cloth is stretched across the top to show that the event, to which the icon corresponds, occurred indoors.

The concept of correspondence is also the basis of the veneration of icons. Precisely because icons correspond to the person or event depicted, whatever veneration is given to icons is understood as being passed on to the prototype. This view was already formulated in the fourth century by St. Basil the Great (*Letters on the Holy Spirit*, 18), and quoted by St. John of Damascus in the eighth century (*First Apology Against Those Who Attack the Divine Images*, 21), when he championed the position of the Orthodox iconodules (icon-venerators) against the iconoclasts (icon-smashers). The Orthodox defenders of the veneration of icons vigorously maintained that it is not the material substance that is venerated, but the prototype; it is not the material substance of Christ, the saints or sacred events that is depicted in icons, but their cosmic, spiritual significance and reality.

16. *St. John the Theologian in Silence, Russian icon, 16th century; in the Kremlin Icon Museum, Suzdal.*

Whereas most authentic Orthodox icons are characterized by a stylistically-achieved silence, the Apostle, St. John the Theologian (the Evangelist), is the only saint of whom there exists an icon type designated: "in silence." This is because the Word of God is so loud and so sublime in John's writings, the Church recognizes that he must have achieved great silence; only when one can quiet the roaring noise of one's ego, mind and senses, can one hear the Divine Voice as fully as St. John did. The way in which the Apostle holds his hand to his mouth conveys a deep meditative silence, during which the Holy Spirit illumined him and directed his writing.

Orthodox spirituality emphasizes the importance of quieting one's inner noise, especially through the constant repetition of the Jesus Prayer. Certainly, St. John the Theologian could well understand how eloquently an icon, a flower, a poem, beauty and silence can speak about the sublime, Divine Word.

17. Cathedral of the Ascension, Yelets, Russia, 19th century.

There are countless treasures of Russian Orthodox spiritual and artistic genius such as this exquisite "working" cathedral, which are a vital part of Russian life, but which foreigners rarely experience.

Standing on a hill overlooking a river, these blues domes ascend heavenward, visible from afar, still serving the age-old function of reminding people of life's purpose and meaning, and inspiring people to make the spiritual ascent of the soul.

The exterior colors - sky-blue with gold domes and light green walls - are carried over into the interior decoration, whose splendor rivals any of the well-known and well-documented monuments of Russian church architecture. Originally constructed in the 19th century, the main church is a traditional cubical cross-in-square with triple apses, whose large interior space opens up into a beautiful dome. Although Western Baroque stylistic elements are obvious, they have been blended with traditional forms in a distinctively Russian way.

Yelets had been home to a very large women's monastery. There is still a community of nuns in the city, and they perform all the functions of altar servers and readers at this cathedral.

5

ARCHITECTURE

RUSSIAN CHURCHES

Jubilantly you prance
Across the Russian skies
Sculpted fanciful fantasies
You leap for joy
Dancing in the Presence

Your colorful cupolas
Stretch longingly heavenward
Like spirit-filled tongues of flame
Filled with the fiery Presence
Which scarcely can you contain

You paint the myriad colors of divine Love
With your many-hued facades
And your many jeweled crowns
You bedeck the hallowed, hollowed spaces
With blue and golden balls

You create a majestic microcosm
For the Uncreated Creator of all
In you primordial Love finds expression
In you the mysteries of the cosmos are incarnate
In you the Holy Mysteries are manifested

You express the Inexpressible
You contain the Uncontainable
You define the Indefinable
You limit the Limitless
You dance in the Presence

5

ARCHITECTURE

The architecture of (Russian) Orthodox churches, or *temples* as they are usually called in Russia, creates a sacred environment. This is the sacred space within which Divine Service is performed, and within which the invisible is made visible, the incorporeal made corporeal, and where He, Who cannot be contained, dwells. Much of what we have already said about liturgy and icons applies equally to sacred architecture. The correspondence between earthly and heavenly realms is crucial in architecture, for the temples are microcosms, wherein temporal sacred rituals correspond to cosmic reality and assume cosmic significance.

Orthodox church architecture characteristically includes the use of a large central dome over the main inner, usually square space, customarily, in conjunction with smaller domes and semi-domes, to signify the coming together of the two realms - heaven (round dome) and earth (square or rectangle). The height of Russian churches rarely exceeds its width or length, especially prior to the seventeenth century, in order that the architectural and liturgical space may convey the principle that humanity and the earth ascend up towards the Divine, at the same time as the Divine descends and makes Itself manifest to those in the earth sphere. The emphasis has always been on the central space under the dome, where heaven and earth are conjoined. Suspended from this large dome over the central space is almost always a sizable cut-glass or metal chandelier, as beautiful as can be afforded. This chandelier represents the beauty of the divine illumination which God sends down to enlighten the world. Domes are universal symbols of the cosmos, the heavens and the divine space, because they are circular and are miniatures of what an unobstructed view of the sky looks like to us. Thus, since the heavens symbolize the dwelling-place of the Divine, so likewise, earthly domes create sacred space wherein the Divine dwells and is manifested. (Naturally, when we speak of God's dwelling-place, we are speaking metaphorically, not literally, because, of course, God cannot be confined to any one place. But, precisely bcause God transcends all time and space, He can also manifest Himself in any and all times and spaces.) Domes also duplicate the shapes of our heads, signifying that we too are microcosms, and temples of the divine in-dwelling Spirit. Just as humans are recognized as being icons of God because we are made in His Image, so our bodies are also regarded as temples of the Divine (Corinthians 6:19), surmounted by miniature cosmic domes - our heads.

The Divine Liturgy and icons correspond to their spiritual prototypes; likewise, churches also correspond to their spiritual prototypes. The Orthodox temple is modeled on the Jewish Temple, and its prototype, the tabernacle of Moses, which was built according to its heavenly prototype, following the very specific directions that God gave to Moses about how the Tabernacle was to be built. Just as the three sub-

18. Church of the Kazan Icon of the Mother of God (Kazan-skaya), Voronezh, Russia, rebuilt in 1988; view from the south.

Rebuilt for the commemoration in 1988 of 1,000 years of Christianity in Russia, this church is an example of the type of reconstruction of churches that has been occurring in Russia in recent years. While showing many traditional characteristics, it is also quite distinctive. Rather than being plastered and painted, as is common, this church has kept the natural red brick, offset with contrasting white trim and green "tent" roofs, with blue cupolas and gold stars.

In this popular five-dome design, the four corner cupolas represent the four Evangelists, and the large central dome represents Christ. Also typical is the square central space, surmounted by the central dome, forming a microcosm, where heaven (domes/cupolas) are united with earth (square). These forms visually affirm the basic theological principle that God became man so that humans may be restrored to union with God. At the west end is the bell tower, connected to the main interior space. Bells have a significant liturgical function, and are a customary part of the Russian church architectural ensemble.

19. Church of the Ascension, Kolomenskoye, Moscow, 1530-2.

The Grand Princes of Moscow had a lovely summer residence on a hill outside Moscow, overlooking the Moskva River, where they expressed in an innovative way the growing pride in Russian culture and national identity that developed as Moscow's power grew in the 15th and 16th centuries. Here, for the first time, the centuries-old Russian wooden architectural forms (see Illustration 21) were boldly translated into masonry, including: the huge octagonal tent-roof; the surrounding galleries and staircases; and the second story elevation of the church over a ground-level 'basement.' The result is a very unusual upward thrust that is enhanced by the eight sets of triple, pointed *kokoshniki*. Aptly dedicated to the Ascension of Christ, no previous Russian church had ever been so vigorously vertical.

The Kolomenskoye preserve, with its two churches, has been returned to the Orthodox Church, and a convent has been officially established.

sequent Jewish Temples in Jerusalem (the last of which was destroyed in the year 70 C.E. (A.D.) by the Roman Emperor, Titus) had three main divisions, so also, the Orthodox temple has three main sections (Illustration 20). The most sacred part of the Jewish Temple was at the eastern end (the direction of the rising sun is universally regarded as sacred) - the *Holy of Holies* - which represented God's dwelling place on earth. It was separated by walls with the veil (curtain) of the temple covering the central holy doors. The Holy of Holies contained the *Ark of the Covenant*, which held (until they disappeared) the tablets of the Ten Commandments - a visible, tangible manifestation of the Divine Presence. So likewise, the Orthodox temple's Holy of Holies is in the easternmost part, usually in a curved apse area, with a dome or semi-dome on top. In this area is located the altar - simultaneously representing the throne and tomb of Christ - upon which stands the *tabernacle* that contains the consecrated Body and Blood of Christ (Illustration 6). Thus, the Orthodox Holy of Holies also contains a visible, tangible manifestation of the Divine Presence. Only the clergy and altar servers are allowed in this area, in recognition of the awe, mystery and unapproachable nature of the holy. This Holy of Holies (sanctuary) is also separated by a screen or wall, covered with icons (the *iconostasis*), pierced by three doors: the *Holy Doors* or *Royal Gates* in the center, and deacons' doors to the left and right (north and south) (Illustration 4).

Among the frescoes in the synagogue in the ancient Syrian city of Dura-Europas, built prior to 256 C.E. and discovered in the 1930's, is a fascinating representation of the Jewish Temple, constructed like a Greek temple, with three sets of doors, and with the Temple curtain over the central door. There are amazing similarities between this third-century Jewish painting of the Temple, and second and third century Christian church architecture that has been excavated in Syria.

In the Jewish Temple, only the high priest was allowed to enter the Holy of Holies, and then, only once a year, on the Day of Atonement. When Christ was crucified, the Gospels say that the veil of the Temple was split apart. (Matthew 27:51. For the full biblical discussion about Christ as the High Priest and sacrifices in the Temple, see Hebrews 7:1 - 10:18, and elsewhere.) This signifies that Christ, as the heavenly High Priest, now reveals the Divine at every Divine Liturgy. This revelation is enacted liturgically when the veil is pulled back, and the deacon, priest or bishop comes through Holy Doors to read the Gospel, to preach the sermon, and to bring the Holy Communion to the people. This is an important symbol, where architecture and ritual are intertwined. The Holy Doors/Royal Gates symbolize the interpenetration between the two worlds - the eternal and temporal, the divine and human, the nonmaterial and material, the invisible and visible (Illustrations 4 & 5).

The second main division of space in the Jewish Temple was the Holy Place, where the altar of sacrifice was located, and where the priests offered sacrifices. In the Orthodox Church, the altar is moved into the Holy of Holies, (Illustration 6) and sacrifice becomes a regular part of Christian life, as the people participate and cooperate with God in the celebration of the divine cosmic sacrifice. Sacrifice is no longer just something people offer to God: God also participates in the sacrifices and offers Himself to the faithful. Most of the second or middle area of the Orthodox temple is where the people stand, under the cosmic dome of heaven. (The Western architectural

20. *Church of the Resurrection, from the Village of Patakino,*
Museum of Wooden Architecture, Suzdal, 1776.

A number of surviving Russian wooden churches have been
moved to museums of wooden architecture. Because the wooden
techniques and forms changed little over the centuries, we can
see in the surviving structures from the 16th through the 20th
centuries what earlier wooden buildings were like.

This simple, rectangular church clearly illustrates the traditional divisions of Orthodox temple architecture. At the east
end is the *apse* or altar area; in the middle, under the central
dome of heaven, is the *nave*, where the people stand; at the west
end is the *narthex* or vestibule, the bell-tower and entrance
porch.

In masonry churches, the apse is usually rounded. In wooden
churches, the rectangle is rounded off by adding one or two additional sides, which in turn, enables the roof to become curved
at the east end. The transition from the square central space to
the cupola is made by an octagonal drum and roof, a motif re-
peated for the bell tower with its "tent" roof.

21. Church of the Nativity of the Mother of God, from the Village of Peredki, Vitoslavlitsy Museum of Wooden Architecture, Novgorod, Russia, before 1539.

One of the oldest extant wooden churches in Russia, and of quite elaborate proportions, the large central space under the octagonal drum and tent roof in this church is expanded by the four equal arms of the Greek-cross plan. The sizable tent roof is covered with 'fish-scale' or 'leaf-like' wooden shingles, that glisten like silver. The church is elevated over a ground level *basement*, and is reached by a covered staircase. Surrounding three sides of the second level is a bench-lined, covered *gallery*. It is precisely this type of pyramidal tent-roof church, with covered galleries and stairs, which were translated into masonry in Moscow in the *Church of the Ascension* at Kolomenskoye (Illustration 19) and *St. Basil's Cathedral* in Red Square (Illustration 24).

erm is *nave*, from the Latin word for *ship*.) This area represents the world in the process of being restored to the Divine Image, and where the Divine Reality is already manifested in the world. There are also special areas in front of the iconostasis and under the central dome and chandelier that are set apart for liturgical action - a type of *sacred stage*, with the icons serving as *sacred scenery*, whereupon the cosmic drama of the sanctification of the world occurs.

The symbolically rich interplay between ritual, iconography and architectural sacred space constantly demonstrates the interpenetration of the heavenly and earthly, divine and human realms, as the liturgical action moves back and forth from the hidden space of the Holy of Holies behind the iconostasis, to the visible space within the middle of the faithful, beneath the unifying dome of heaven.

The third part of the Jewish Temple was the outer court, where the people stood. In the Orthodox temple, the third area today is small, usually called in English a *vestibule* or *narthex*. This represents the unredeemed world - the world apart from God or outside the Kingdom of God. The rites of Baptism and Chrismation start here, signifying the leaving of the unredeemed world, and the entering into the realm that is in the process of sanctification - the main body of the temple, unified under a single large dome of heaven.

The *standing-in-two-worlds*, of which we have spoken before, is graphically depicted in church architecture. The altar area represents the divine realm; the vestibule represents the outer realm, apart from God. The area between them is where the opposites are reconciled and brought together; it is the place where we stand in two worlds - physically, liturgically, spiritually, theologically and aesthetically. It is the place where the invisible is made visible in the icons that cover the walls and ceilings and iconostasis. Through the icons, through the Divine Service, and through the liturgical action that comes through the doors of the iconostasis, the divine manifestation enters the realm where we stand.

Russian Orthodox architecture and iconography is not just something external and removed from daily life: the Orthodox faithful are part of their church temple in a very real, personal and individual way. Just as each Orthodox home is regarded as being a small temple, so too, do our heads form the domes of the temples of our bodies, wherein dwells the Divine Presence. The architecture and the individual spirituality are two dimensions of the same reality, namely, that each individual is called to recognize his or her inherent nature - and that of every other human being - as being a sanctified temple of the Divine Image and Likeness. Each human is thus called to follow the example of the Virgin Mary - the Blessed Birthgiver of God (*Theotokos*)- who is referred to as a "sanctified temple and spiritual paradise," whose very body was made into a throne, and whose womb was "made more spacious than the heavens" (*Hymn to the Theotokos*, St. Basil's Liturgy).

Russian spirituality puts great emphasis on seeing the Divine in persons, especially in the poor, the prisoner, the hungry, the thirsty. What is the path to salvation? It is seeing Christ in the eye of the dome of every person's head, and acting in accord with the Christ within us by feeding the hungry, clothing the naked, welcoming the stranger and visiting the sick and imprisoned, as though the person were Christ Himself. Russian Orthodox spirituality takes very seriously Christ's injunction that "if you have done it (feed the hungry, etc.) to one of the least of my brothers, you have done it to me (Matthew 25:35-40).

One way in which this spirituality and theology is translated architecturally and iconographically is not only by having Christ the Pantocrator (Almighty) depicted in the central dome (that reminds us that Christ dwells within the dome of each of the temples that are our bodies), but also by portraying the Theotokos (Virgin Mary) above the altar, in the half-dome that physically unites the curved upper cosmic space, with the lower closer-to-earth space of the physical temple, thus symbolically uniting the earth with the heavens. The church temple is thus something far more than an empty, cold, stone or wooden building - it is an organic, alive body and temple of the Divine Presence.

Church architecture embodies the same theological, moral and spiritual principles as do the icons and Divine Service. It is entirely appropriate to be speaking of moral precepts when speaking of temple architecture; if the theology in space, shape, color, stone and wood which is Russian church architecture did not embody the same spiritual, theological and moral vision of the Gospels, icons and Divine Service, then there would be something deficient, and the supposed sacred space would not be sacred. To stand in sacred space is to become aware of the moral imperative that is the consequence of standing in the Divine Presence.

The placement or *program* of the numerous icons in the Orthodox temple follows the symbolic principle of the correspondence between the celestial, cosmic reality and its earthly temporal manifestation, in accordance with the ancient dictum: "As above, so below." This reflects the vital Orthodox principle of the unity of the visible and invisible worlds, divine and human, spiritual and material, and the view of salvation as the actualization of that unity, which is the process of *theosis* (deification or sanctification).

We have thus far focused on the meaning and significance of the sculpting of *interior* sacred space of Russian Orthodox temple architecture, as a setting for the sacred drama of Divine Service and manifestation of the Divine Presence, and we have seen how the thirteen spiritual-theological principles of Russian Orthodox religion are to be discerned in Orthodox Divine Service, icons and church architecture. We will now consider a few aspects of the *exterior* sculpting of Russian church architecture.

The transfiguration and sanctification of matter, the organic unity of the natural, human and divine realms, and a certain paradoxical playfulness, exuberance and joyfulness of the resurrection of life are characteristics of much of the exterior appearance of Russian temple architecture.

The earliest churches in ancient *Rus* (the original name for Russia) were made of wood; thus, naturally, they have not survived, although there are literary references and descriptions of them. The oldest stone (brick) temples are adapted from Byzantine architectural styles. They are frequently cubes, with a trefoil-shaped apse at the east end, usually with one, five, seven or thirteen domes. Sometimes they have some decoration in the patterns of the brickwork. The broader, flatter Byzantine dome was gradually supplanted by the distinctive Russian 'onion' dome. The Russian 'onion' dome cupolas are like tongues of fire of the Holy Spirit and

22. *Church of the Transfiguration of Christ, from the Village of Kozlyatiyevo, Museum of Wooden Architecture, Suzdal, Russia, 1756.*

There are two important wooden architectural forms in this church: the "weddding-cake" type central dome, and the double-curved, pointed *ogee* gables or *botchi*, that echo the shape of onion domes. The three-tiered "wedding-cake" dome visualizes the important Orthodox emphasis on the ascent of the soul, as on a ladder, to the divine realm, while yet remaining a part of the organic unity of the Body of Christ. This journey of the soul, symbolized in the shape of the Orthodox temple, is especially clear here: the spiritual aspirant "lays aside all earthly cares" (bottom level), and ascends through the celestial spheres (3 tiers), in order to arrive at the goal - transfiguration and union with God (the top cupola).

Further emphasizing the upward ascent of the soul are the pointed, *ogee* gables. Because they look like flames, they also symbolize the means and result of becoming transfigured: being filled with the fire of the Holy Spirit, and the fiery divine Love that consumes and purifies.

23. Church of the Transfiguration of Christ, Island of Kizhi, Lake Onega, Karelia, Russia, 1714.

The experience of the soul's journey on the path of resurrection, ascension, descent of the Holy Spirit and transfiguration is most poignantly visualized in this testimony of the spiritual vision and skill of Russian Orthodox 'folk' artists. By far the most spectacular of all surviving wooden churches, this 22-cupola temple is very aptly dedicated to the Transfiguration of Christ; the forms themselves are an evocation of transfiguration - the goal of Orthodox spiritual life.

There is here a Greek-cross floor plan, modified into an octagon, from which cascading cupolas and *ogee* gables ascend, to culminate in a large single cupola at top. The multiplicity of cupolas, whose shape is echoed in the *ogee* gables, intensify the sense of organic, up-surging energy. On each of the 4 levels, radiating upwards from the 4 arms of the cross-plan, there is an *ogee* gable and cupola, with an additional gable and cupola on the diagonals. The 22nd cupola is over the altar.

like the intense fiery fervor of Russian spirituality. The purity of the white-washed cube with its golden dome(s) was, and still is an ever-present reminder of the Divine Presence in the midst of daily life.

The most distinctive exterior elements of Russian architecture are derived from its folk tradition of wooden architecture, where homes and church share many similar forms and decorative motifs. In some regions, such as Siberia, where wood is still the most available building material, church and domestic architecture built today looks much the same as it did many centuries ago.

One of the most spectacular examples of extant wooden architecture is the *Church of the Transfiguration*, built in 1714 on the island of Kizhi in Lake Onega, about 250 miles northeast of St. Petersburg, in the Karelian region (Illustration 23 and and the cover). It is constructed entirely of wood, without a single nail. What makes this church so spectacular is its twenty-two onion-dome cupolas, each covered with shingles (hand-cut with an axe), that are like fish-scales or leaves. The effect is a fantastic sculptured fantasy of shapes and textures, that is ever changing, as shadow and light constantly move across the multitude of surfaces. It is like a sculpted poem or dancing song that affirms that beauty, joy, love are what life is about. It shares the same vision as Orthodox iconography: true life is a transfigured spiritual life, in which matter and soul are both deified. The Kizhi *Transfiguration Church* is an ideal example of how a temple manifests the Kingdom of God already appearing on earth, where the faithful stand in two worlds.

This church on Kizhi Island is also a statement about the importance of fantasy, imagination and playfulness of spirit as a quality of being human, and as a quality of spirituality that springs from the perception of creation as the play and dance of God - a playing and dancing and laughing God. The Kizhi church also proclaims the unity of life, wherein the reconciliation of opposites is both feasible and desirable. It is an expression of the harmony and balance of many opposing forces: nature and humanity, God and humanity, imagination and technology, right-brain and left-brain, male and female, life and death, dark and light, east and west. Kizhi is organic, living, vibrant, at one with nature, a cooperative endeavor between humans and the natural, cosmic order. The wood is dead, yet alive, infused with a life-force energy that declares that death is a misnomer. Dedicated to the Transfiguration of Christ, the Kizhi temple is a visible affirmation that the material world can be transfigured, that matter is good, not evil, and that we humans are a part of nature, and are intended to live in harmony with it, not subdue and exploit it.

Some elements of the *Transfiguration Church* of Kizhi are similar to those in the most famous example of wooden architectural forms translated into stone - the *St. Basil's/Protection Cathedral* in Moscow's Red Square, built by Ivan IV in the mid-sixteenth century. Perhaps it is very appropriate that this structure is used by Soviets and Westerners alike to represent the Soviet Union, and especially the Russian Republic: it exemplifies the Russian sense of beauty, fantasy, imagination, playfulness, the merging of cultures (Asian, European, Byzantine and Slavic), and the unity or conciliarity (*sobornost*) of life lived in two worlds.

24. Cathedral of St. Basil the Blessed-Protection of the Mother of God (Pokrov), Red Square, Moscow, 1555-60; Barma and Postnik, architects.

For most people, St. Basil's is the most readily identifiable symbol of Russia. It may be said that it speaks of the Russian playful sense of imagination, fantasy, exuberance, and the power of spiritual transformation. The church was built by Ivan IV, the "Terrible," to commemorate his victory over the Mongol Tartars at Kazan in 1552.

St. Basil's is one of the early churches in Moscow to translate into masonry the distinctive motifs of centuries-old traditions of wooden architecture, especially: the large, pyramidal 'tent' roof over the central interior space; cascading *kokoshniki* (rounded and pointed flat gable motifs); a basement at ground level, with the church elevated over it, reached by staircases that feed into the covered galleries on three sides.

The plan consists of a central church, with eight chapels around it, under each of the cupolas. The variegated onion domes were added later on in the 16th century, and the colorful painted decorative patterns in the 17th century.

Before concluding, let us say a few words about the changing condition of church architecture today in the former Soviet republics. Only a small fraction of the churches that existed prior to the Bolshevik Revolution of 1917 still stand, and most of the best of those that survived have been used as museums, if they were not used as warehouses, factories, nightclubs, swimming pools, or just left to deteriorate. The situation has changed radically now, as a result of Gorbachev's policies, the 1988 commemoration of the Millennium (1,000 years) of Christianity in Russia, and the democratization and independence of the former Soviet republics. One thousand new churches were opened in 1988, and 2,185 new parishes registered in just the first nine months of 1989. New churches open every single day. Many former temples and monasteries have been returned to the Church and renovated or rebuilt, and countless others have been newly built. Renovation and reconstruction are everywhere. Traditional architectural and iconographic styles of different periods are followed in new building projects, and frequently crumbling heaps of bricks are beautifully restored according to the appearance of the previous original temples and monasteries.

Reconstruction and renovation have been a way of life for Russians throughout the centuries, because wooden churches and homes were always burning down or being destroyed by invaders. Today's new temple architecture - whether of wood (in Siberia) or brick, whether simple or ornate, whether early or late style - continues to sculpt matter and space to create a microcosm of the divine indwelling within time and space, within which the process of restoration of the cosmos to divine Beauty is manifested as a present reality.

In this brief introduction to Russian religion, liturgy, icons and architecture we have tried to demonstrate the spiritual, theological and artistic unity of the Russian Orthodox Church, and how vitally alive these art forms still are today. An inquiry into the meaning and interpretation of Russian sacred arts is especially fruitful and rich now, with the resurgence of religion in the republics of the former Soviet Union. Particularly as a result of the celebration in 1988 of the Millennium of Russian Christianity, millions of Russians, Ukrainians, Belorussians, and other Slavic people are rediscovering the rich treasures of their own spiritual and aesthetic heritage. However, since the meaning of Russian sacred arts is universal, (as, indeed, Beauty and Truth are universal), they can speak to and touch the heart of anyone, regardless of national or ethnic heritage, who is searching for Beauty and Truth, and for an understanding of the spiritual principles of life and of the cosmos.

ILLUSTRATIONS

Cover. Detail of domes, *Church of the Transfiguration*, Island of Kizhi, Lake Onega, Karelia, 1714. Photo by author, 1991.

1. (p.6) *Cathedral of the Birthgiver of God,* Monastery of St. Tikhon, Zadonsk, Diocese of Voronezh and Lipetsk, Russia; 18th century; with partial restoration. Photo by author, 1991.

2. (p.8) *Holy Trinity-St. Sergius Lavra Monastery,* Sergieev Posad (formerly Zagorsk), Russia, 14th-19th centuries; panorama from the Southeast. Photo by author, 1989.

3. (p.14) *Cathedral of the Savior,* Savior-Andronikov Monastery, Moscow, 1410-27(?). Photo by author, 1991.

4. (p.25) The iconostasis, *Church of the Fathers of the Seven Ecumenical Councils,* St. Daniel's Monastery, Moscow; painted in 1988 in the 15th century Moscow style. Photo by author, 1989.

5. (p.26) Reading of the Gospel during Divine Liturgy, *Theophany Patriarchal Cathedral,* Moscow, late 18th century, reconstructed in mid-19th century. Photo by author, 1989.

6. (p.33) Altar, *Cathedral of the Protection of the Mother of God (Pokrov),* Voronezh, Russia. Photo by author, 1989.

7. (p.34) Child Receiving Holy Communion, *Protection Cathedral,* Voronezh, Russia. Photo by author, 1989.

8. (p.36) Priest's Vestments, embroidered by Mother Angelina, Yelets, Russia. Photo by author, 1991.

9. (p.38) *Yaroslavl Mother of God,* Russian icon, 2nd half of the 15th century; in the Tretyakov Gallery, Moscow.

10. (p.43) *Ascension of Christ,* Russian icon, late 15th century.

11. (p.44) *Resurrection of Christ,* Russian icon, 15th century.

12. (p.47) *Transfiguration of Christ,* by Theophanes the Greek, Russian icon, ca. 1403; in the Tretyakov Gallery, Moscow.

13. (p.48) *Crucifixion of Christ*, Russian icon, late 14th century; in the Andrei Rublev Museum of Icons, Moscow.

14. (p.51) *Annunciation*, Russian icon, 15th century; from the Protection (Pokrov) Convent, Suzdal.

15. (p.52) *Nativity of Christ*, Russian icon, 16th century; from the Nativity Cathedral, Suzdal.

16. (p.55) *St. John the Theologian in Silence*, Russian icon, 16th century; in the Kremlin Museum of Icons, Suzdal.

17. (p.56) *Cathedral of the Ascension*, Yelets, Russia, 19th century; K. Ton, architect. Photo by author, 1991.

18. (p.61) *Church of the Kazan Icon of the Mother of God (Kazanskaya)*, Voronezh, Russia, rebuilt in 1987. Photo by author, 1989.

19. (p.62) *Church of the Ascension*, Kolomenskoye, Moscow, 1530-32. Photo by author, 1989.

20. (p.65) *Church of the Resurrection*, from the Village of Palakino, Museum of Wooden Architecture, Suzdal, 1776. Photo by author, 1991.

21. (p.66) *Church of the Nativity of the Mother of God*, from the Village of Peredki, Vitoslavlitsy Museum of Wooden Architecture, Novgorod, Russia, before 1539. Photo by author, 1991.

22. (p.71) *Church of Transfiguration of Christ*, from the Village of Kozlyatiyevo, Museum of Wooden Architecture, Suzdal, Russia, 1756. Photo by author, 1991.

23. (p.72) *Church of the Transfiguration of Christ*, Island of Kizhi, Lake Onega, Karelia, Russia, 1714. Photo by author, 1991.

24. (p.75) *Cathedral of St. Basil the Blessed and the Protection of the Mother of God (Pokrov)*, Red Square, Moscow, 1555-60; Barma and Postnik, architects. Photo by author, 1989.

ABOUT THE AUTHOR

The author, Dr. Jane M. de Vyver, has been teaching a wide variety of interdisciplinary humanities, philosophy, religion and cultural history courses at Michigan colleges and universities since 1976, including Marygrove College, Wayne State and Michigan State Universities, and Lawrence Technological University.

Professor de Vyver holds a Bachelor of Arts in Philosophy, Religion and French; a Masters of Theology seminary degree; a Masters in Art History; and a Ph.D. in Art History, Religion and Philosophy.

Her main scholarly interests are Russian arts, religion and culture, and the interdisciplinary interpretation of the arts. She is developing a major television documentary series, *Russian Treasures*, which will bring to life the magnificent 1000+ year history of Russian arts and ideas. In addition to making videos and writing books about Russian life and culture, the author is also producing professional video programming for pan-Orthodox Christian education and television broadcasting.

Printed and bound for Firebird Publishers by
Harlo Printing Company
50 Victor Avenue, Detroit, MI 48203